BIRD
LIGHT

Saint Julian Press

Poetry

PRAISE for BIRD LIGHT

"Here is an exquisite collection of lyrical and imagistic poems firmly rooted in the natural world. But Elizabeth Cohen's poems are also rooted in the human, referring in an oblique way to loss and sorrow, joy and love. This is truly a beautiful book about survival and the way the natural world helps to heal us."

~ Maria Mazziotti Gillan
American Book Award Winner

"One of the few things as great as watching birds is watching birds through the eyes of a masterful poet. Elizabeth Cohen is just that—her craft so fine and so smooth that I read one of the poems twice before realizing it was a villanelle. Combine this meticulous, honed craft with the abandon and whimsy of a keen, playful intellect, and you have verse that sings and dips and soars as gracefully and naturally as a bird in flight. *Bird Light* is a book that "licks the air," "flings, madly, like a shot punctuation mark," and 'leaps branches and telephone wires to ride the air to an invisible height.' Here is a poetic and avian treasure."

~Melissa Studdard, author of
I Ate the Cosmos for Breakfast and *Six Weeks to Yehidah*

"These poems fluidly move between memory and a present experience of time, place, love, loss, and death while gently reminding readers that sophisticated treatment of these large ideas is a treasure to be sought, a pleasure that Cohen seeks and shares with us. Here are poems full of grace and quiet power."

~ Catherine Daly, author of *Locket* and *To Delete and Instruct*

"Elizabeth Cohen's *Bird Light* is a wonder and a delight, a kind of autobiography in birds, filled with exuberance and driven by an intimate, passionate, quirky engagement with the world."

~ Cecilia Woloch, NEA Fellow and author of
Carpathia, Late, Sacrifice, Earth and other works

"Elizabeth Cohen reminds me of Anne Porter, Jimmy Schuyler, Joe Stroud, Gary Snyder, and Mary Oliver (a mighty visionary company, I think). She knows not only the names of living things; she knows what it means to live. A poetic field-guide to the poet's world, *Bird Light* is a book whose whole keeps the reader "in the middle of beautiful/in the middle of glorious.""

~ Mark Statman, author of
A Map of the Winds , *That Train Again*, and other works

"Layering disparate voices –from the colloquially humorous to the quietly elegiac–Elizabeth Cohen creates three-dimensional moments of reckoning. Reading *Bird Light*, we find ourselves within the constant swerves of avian flight and song, and, with almost unbearable accuracy, within the urgent emotions of our own lives."

~ Celia Bland, Associate Director, Institute for Writing
& Thinking at Bard College, and the author of *Soft Box*

"*Bird Light* is a bird phenomenology. Birds are embodiments of time or disembodiments of time. They are characters that are funny and annoying, loyal and everything beautiful, charming and irresistible, sad and even scary. They are surprising joy, new life, and they disappear into another world as our beloved dead do. Elizabeth Cohen's poetry is a phenomenon, a witty consciousness, all that birds are and all that they carry us beyond."

~ Aliki Barnstone, Poet Laureate of Missouri,
author of *Blue Earth*, *Wild With It* and *Dwelling*

"Elizabeth Cohen's poems are swerving birds, with wings shaped like punctuation marks, travelling between ornithology and memory. Beautiful, original, and full of casual surprises, with the utmost verve and grace."

~ Gillian McCain, author of *Tilt*, and *Religion*, co-author of
Please Kill Me: The Uncensored Oral History of Punk, among other works

BIRD
LIGHT

Poems

by

Elizabeth Cohen

SAINT JULIAN PRESS
HOUSTON

Published by

SAINT JULIAN PRESS, INC.

2053 Cortlandt, Suite 200
Houston, Texas 77008

www.saintjulianpress.com

ISBN-13: 978-0-9965231-9-6
ISBN: ISBN-10: 0-9965231-9-7
Library of Congress Control Number: 2016948819

COVER & INTERIOR ART: ALIKI BARNSTONE

TITLES: AIR DANCE & BIRD LIGHT

AUTHOR PHOTO: TORUNN LYNGROTH ABERLE

—for Ava, who will forever be my little bird, my light.

ALL TIME AT ONCE

CONTENTS

COUNTERSINGING

HABITAT

CREPUSCULAR

MURMURATION

SKYLARKING

FIELD MARKS

PLUMAGE

MIGRATION

INDENTIFIABLE MARKINGS

"MEANWHILE THE WILD GEESE, HIGH IN THE CLEAN BLUE AIR,
ARE HEADING HOME AGAIN."

—MARY OLIVER

BIRD
LIGHT

COUNTERSINGING

BIRD FIELD

RED CRESTED FLICKER

Don't be surprised if you scare one up from the ground.
They like it down there with the beetles, which they spoon up
so cleverly with their rounded beaks. You would think
they would be ensconced in trees, pecking bark, but no,
they prefer the ant in the sand, the shiny pebble in the creek.
In the east they go all about in their bright yellow shawls,
but head west and you will find them dolled up in lipstick
like your mother. When I was little, I called them Diaper Birdies,
on account of the bright white flash of their rumps. Emily,
who lived on the next street, called them Made-in-Japans,
because of the way they could seem almost plastic, holding so still,
as if posing for some bird photographer always about to arrive.

FESTIVAL OF THE CRANES

Close your eyes and listen.
It is the sound of hard rain,
occasional car doors slamming.

There is an actual wind,
bird wind, that starts up.
Take the Rachel Carson tour

Through the blizzard of sandhills
and whoopings, heads raised and long legs
dropped down, like a billion semicolons

in action. Saying pause, please,
observe this clapping, singing festival,
wrapping the sky in grey

at the Bosque del Apache
National Wildlife Refuge
not far from where my best friend's

brother went to prison for a decade.
Not far from the place our truck broke,
pulled right off its chassis

by the weight of a boat, in eleventh
grade. Now her brother is a gardener
for a university. The boy who owned that

yellow truck sells used cars on Fourth Street
in Albuquerque. The world recovers,
just look at this:

The rise and rise and rise of a species,
like the ground itself has decided to fly.
Not far from heaven, really, if heaven is a place

where things lift up
by some internal power
and move on with their lives

OWL CAM

1.

The female Great Horned Owl
laid the first egg of the season
on the morning of January 23, 2016.
It sat with attitude in the nest
like that first cake laid down
at the cakewalk, perfect
and perfectly made
and she, beside it. proud baker,
ruffling her wings.
Last year the first egg
(of two) was laid on January 1st
as if to inaugurate the year,
set it on a right course.
The female sat pacifically, incubating,
and receiving food from the male,
little bits of unidentifiable
meat or bread from the garbage
at the rest stop down the road.
Check out this video
of the male coming in with a lizard
last summer. The female stands up
providing a nice view of the egg
she laid on June 22nd.
It glows beneath her, special
as a rare comet that had to come
through her to get to the earth.

2.

Great Horned Owls can lay anywhere
from one to four eggs, any time of the year,
but two eggs is the most common clutch size.
Two eggs is fine. It is the magic number
of laying, really, the creation of nest buddies,
or maybe even lifelong companions, like these.

POND CAM

Here is a real view
from the Cornell Lab Pond Cam
at Sapsucker Woods

As you can see
the mallards are courting
by the lilies' edge

As you can see
the wind is having a good time
in the trees

As you can see
there has been a lovely party
on the mud beach

The duck prints
are still at it
a one step, two step

Cutie Alert!
Black capped chickadee
in the maple stand

And now you can count them:
one two three four five
mourning doves
lined up and preening
on a single branch

GLOSSY IBIS, SPURWINK RIVER
~ *After Bill Roorbach*

There is something about the curvature of beak
just a bit, at the tip, in the soporific light
An ancient needle designed to sew a leak

In the world, or catch an escaped streak
of gold, an insect glancing off the marsh, so bright
There is something about the curvature of beak

A call resounds, it's ibis doublespeak
A compadre answers her with also quite
An ancient needle designed to sew a leak

They're singing back and forth, its hide and seek
With lullabies of swish grass to delight
There is something about the curvature of beak

So regal, truly anyone would speak
Of the grandeur of this creature here, this sight
An ancient needle designed to sew a leak

Ready to repair God's tapestry, a tweak
In the universe's dark and broke-toothed night
There is something about the curvature of beak
An ancient needle designed to mend a leak

HABITAT

SUN FARM PRAIRIE

THE YES

woke up to the other side
smell of the crunch and cobble of late grass
bloom the morning

smell of over
smell of early

had a glass of chilled maybe
with some toasted perhaps

the lace dress of the frost looking so very
and now the dancing
now the swaying

AFTER THE AFTER

the small green things
and even smaller orange things
tossed up their skirts and spun in the light
flaunting the shadows of their silver tightropes

then the yellow stick things started bragging
their hearts full of purple
they, too, did the most outlandish dance
the dew there, quivering

each drop with its own personal rainbow
each drop saying
quite clearly
here is where you are

AREA CODES

Dear 505, you were mesa
and chaff

roadrunners on the river bed
cottonwood's crag

607 and 518
little shack

in the 203, there is
no going back

You're all just numbers now
nostalgia cows

herded along Tunnel Road
in the dawn mist

902, 212, you are where it all began
true love and loss of love, the kissed

and the kisser,
when Jack the Ripper

sawed through my ankle
and left me stich-zippered

Dear 505, wash over me
with that special recipe

of your warm red dust, let me sit
in the sift

of slow light
let me live in the scurry and drift

of roadrunner time
dig in

my other heel
the good one

ZIP CODES

1.
87111, my beginning
Your spinning dust and pick-up trucks
goat heads in my toes

13833, I was nothing but a shmata
in your exhausted hand
lost between two generations of filth

I earned my way to you, 06812
with your exquisite icebar of trust
Your nestlings on the porch
The favorite cat, buried by the mailbox

2.
Here I sit in the lap of you
12901
There is still a little kick in me
a little bite back, a little dare

you are my last chance, truly
with your honeysuckle air

12901, you with your Northern Flicker
and lone grackles that cat call and swear

BIRDLESS

Maybe it has happened to someone you know
Someone lucky, who once lived
beneath a migratory path of cranes

But something broke, left them birdless
stranded in the grey light of 2:00 am Gunsmoke
in the company of the hawkers of special mops
their lucky lives blown wildly off course

Maybe it happened to you
Your life unzipped from your toes
like the charwoman's shadow
Your farm in foreclosure and the baby
grown into a woman who never calls

leaving you alone in the 3:00 am
flicker of detective shows
and frenetic tap dancers at 4:36
not a bird in sight
Just watch the houses from the night train
and you will see they are lit from within
by the blue cube glow of Cheers
and earthquake news from other lands

It happened to me. The Robin Redbreast
the mud swallows on the porch
egrets in the field   the polysyllabic jays
the velvet scrimshaw of my nights etched with bats
all replaced by infinite changeable things

Everyone, everywhere, sleeping with television

CREPUSCULAR

CLOUD TREE

BIRD ELIXIR

It was a crow convention
very political
with crow speeches
crow sit-ins
even a crow moment-of-silence
followed by a jamboree of crow
with much dancing and merriment

They feasted on day-old Dunkin's
and someone's cast off Mcburger and fries

The sun glanced off
their onyx wings
they threw their shadows down like spent napkins
and the wind was full of crow
the water spoke of nothing but crow

Dinner got cold
the football game was neglected
children began imitating them
It was frankly adorable

Everyone looked up from laptops
and I-phones
forgetting their plans for Hawaii
the dead soldier, the toxic spill
the Dow Jones Industrial Average

For four whole minutes
crow was everything
and everything was crow

JUNE MOON

a bright and sexy moon
a moss-and-wood-scented
starry-eyed moon

once it got unstuck from that big tree
it went wild -- swaying and waving, samba
on the dance floor of Squantz Pond

then that snowy owl came out to take
a great U-turn over the water
throwing down her wide moon shadow
saying "hey mama hey mama hey mama look at me mama"

so we do

IN THE MEAN TIME

embittered, recalcitrant ship of wind
stopped by on its way to Canada
disrespectfully k-o'ed two elderly backyard trees
then sobbed all over the yard like a baby
before chugging away
leaving this calling card:

a single, shiny upside-down crow
one claw protruding from the hedge

DUNKIN' DUCKLINGS

Friday evening
at the puddle
in the Dunkin' Donuts'
Drive Thru
Plattsburgh, New York, 2016

Somebody's dropped a quarter
which glistens
like a last bit of Thursday

It's on fire
the hatchlings swim
in the oily phosphorescence
toddle behind their mother

To the curb and back
Someone is yelling on their cellphone:
"I don't know why
out of the whole wide world
these ducks pick the Drive Thru

These ducks, these ducks, dammit
they need to get a move on"

THE BOOK OF SPARROW
~ for Julie

In the beginning there was the sparrow
and sparrow light was tossed over the water
and that became dawn
and sparrow shadow flew over the garden
and this was the beginning of dusk
and sparrow flew all around the world
and this created night and day

Sparrow lit upon a pinnacle of rock
and the humans began to burn oil
Sparrow slept in trees
and there was the invention of paper

Soon after arrived the development
of genetically altered wheat
and invasions of displaced species
Valleys were burning
the oceans became confused

Sparrow lifted up on eddies of wind
and rested on the edge of the landfill
where worms were plentiful
Famines and wars and droughts and pestilence
appeared and vanished
and the seasons became weary
and forgot to show up one year

Sparrow opened its wings above
to pull across the blankets of dawn and dusk
and carried a raft of stars on its back

The glaciers were melting by this time
and pods of whales were throwing themselves
upon the shores, with great exertion
There was a Perseid shower of sparrows
some nights, and mornings, a whirling
a sparrow tornado that rose up above the slag
battered the cities and claimed the atmosphere wholly

And sparrow wrote in sparrow hieroglyphics
upon the final days
a sparrow prayer

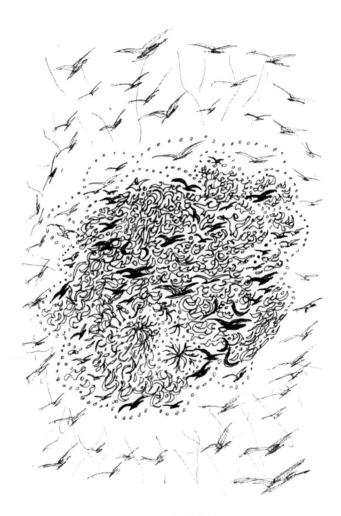

SUN FLIGHT

MURMURATION

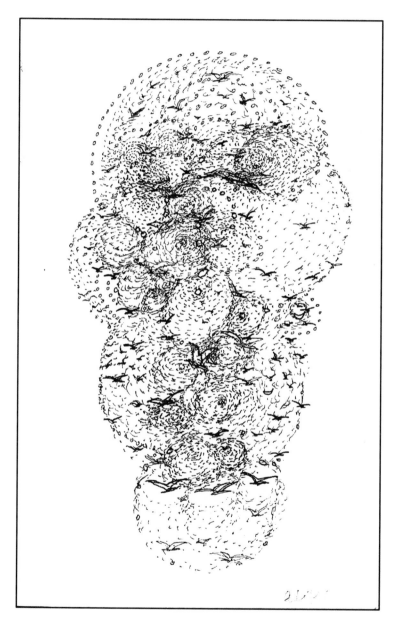

WINGED WORLD

BIRD LIGHT

1.
When my marriage was over
the birds began

First the tiniest--
bullfinch and warbler

Yellow and red confetti
drifting over winter noir

The woodpeckers arrived next
They were so repetitive!

Speaking only of snow
and rain and snow

By summer, hummingbirds helicoptered
the lilacs; I followed

thrusting my whole face inside

2.
Never mistake a raven for a crow
The light off a crow is a darkness

(Back in the winter, they stalked me—
little shreds of lost night)

One thing ends inside your life
and there is an opening for something new

Your eyes start over, widen toward a periphery
When the ravens finally came, in spring

they brought along their blacklight glow
heaven's purple, capes of hope

WHEN I WAS LIGHT, WHEN I WAS WATER, WHEN I WAS THE BLACKBIRD, WHEN I WAS THE BOOT

Here I am, a silver shawl, whipping in the May wind.
Little flecks of fire spark my back and sing.

Here I am, a whitecap on the face of the lake, licking the air.

Here I am, the Blackbird, four feet high and rising
in the dawn-encrusted sky.

Here I am, the bottom of the boot of the man on the motorcycle,
I wait for the light to change so I can toss kisses at the pavement

flashing by.

IN PRAISE OF THE MIDDLE

in the middle of the blue blue
in the middle of the hot hot
in the middle of the honeysuckle air
in the middle of the umbrella tree

in the middle of beautiful
in the middle of glorious
in the middle of the middle

in the middle of the jello, the fruit
in the middle of hiccups, the sneeze

in the middle of the bed, the line, the ninth grade
the book

the soup
the dance
the song

the day at the beach
the wild thing, the kiss

in the middle of the storm of birds, the bee dance

my momma said it best:
the middle is the good part
all the rest is preparation, denouement

DOG WIND

It can hit a mile away, mile-and-a-half on a windy day
When it does, you will not, ever, mistake it
for hay wind, for lake wind
for bird wind, for wind of fish

It is dog wind and you punch the gas
suddenly heated in your sweater of cowardice

that sharp need to escape the caliphate
of loneliness, south of the ASPCA
where you catch it, or it catches you

HAPPINESS

is seven ticks past seven
when you must rise and you know you must rise
to your toast, your books, the toilet bowl plunger
the counter's sponge, the roadside lemonade girls
flying the white innocent flags of their breaths
the unfed cats, the unfed child, the whole unfed city of geese
yet you hardly move
because right then, at seven past seven
is when the starlings murmurate
become a single moving hand
unwrapping the articulated pink bronchia of the trees

BLUEBIRD

When I was twenty-two and heartbroken
I got the tattoo:

A bluebird over my right breast
I imagined was the place

That marked my pain.
Later, I learned my bruised heart

Was lower down
and on the other side.

But that bird didn't care, it has flown with me since,
over skin and blood, ribs and hips,

Days of errands, dream-soaked nights.
It hovered over the death beds of each of my parents,

And for nine months it glided over the soft,
unconnected bones of my daughter's head.

It's left wing tilting from the top
of my nipple, up into the open air.

She often asks to see it now and when she does
I slip down my shirt, my bra, my mother pride.

I peel back my whole life so she can look
at mommy's bird, blurred and dipping now,

still flying across my body toward a place
where it will never arrive.

SKYLARKING

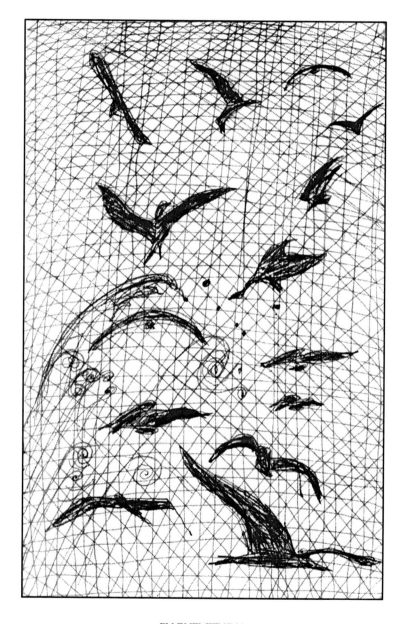

FLIGHT STUDY

THE AFTERLIFE OF BIRDS

I had a dream that I was dreaming
and in the second dream I was pierced by an arrow
you shot in the first dream

But then I had a third dream
without arrows or bows
or all that ruby blood that spilled from me

The third dream was a dream of beautiful dancing
in which there was an abundance of white birds
like the largest snowflakes, falling to the ground

And you said: "Did you see it?"
And I said: "Yes, what a lot of geese"
But you said: "No, I meant my arrow
—the one I killed you with—
(the one that has now transported you
to an afterlife of birds)"

1ST POEM OF SEX AND TIME

is about the rare little moment
about the next and next

hawk light
chickadee light

is about the sudden next and the almost next
the bird and the anti bird

and the dance of crow
and the dance of hip

about the bottom lip
and the next suddenly and the almost next

and the almost and the suddenly
until the maybe soon

and the sudden deep
and the sudden slow until the quick, quick

and the kakopoo
and the florican

and again, the bottom lip, the thigh on foot
and the scent of next

and the harder next
taste of ear   taste of it

of robin breath
ibis crown

nightjar
condor

stork and cuckoo
and the last moment

like the first moment
and it and
it
and it

2ND POEM OF SEX AND TIME

O you, my San Andreas fault, my earthquake, my end zone
my time zone, my space time
my space shuttle ride

my rare sighting of eagle
my rare sighting of hawk

my autumn wren
my begin again

my time is collapsed
my time is bent
my Einsteinian time

my hookah time
my friendly skies

my personal tsunami
my twisted binge

my this is not love
my this is love
my good time
my sweet, sweet time
my oh my oh my oh my
my this is
my is
my

FANCY FREE

1.

Your momma used to say it: *fancy free.*
"What do you think, we can all just be fancy free?
Is this your idea of how to spend your afternoon,
all fancy free?"

Fancy free sounded good, good on top of good.
Fancy, like a wedding cake.
Free like the runaway horse, in the adjacent field,
mane quivering, free like bantering seagulls
that catch eddies and updrafts.

You always think of it on those days
when something is just so lovely it trips into guilt.

Sand between the toes. Massage of the breeze.
Fancy free.
Double feature at the movies
with candy and soda
and more candy and soda

just because.
Fancy free.

2.

Double cartwheels in the lake, perfectly videoed with the i-phone
when both girls were playing hooky and you, you let them, bad momma.
Fancy, fancy, fancy free.

THE COUGH

is a migrating bird that returns
each season for another round

it rises, exalted, from her throat
a lark from her lips, a wreck of gulls

bellows from her belly
like bullfinches

casts about her like a falcon
then waltzes her to sleep, in pretty fits

flamboyant as a flamingo
sometimes it gaggles like up-high geese

and even charms, cute as a goldfinch
or hummingbird

it has traveled many places
gone to camp, it loves the sea

it is the party of jays
the boil of hawks

the deceit of the lapwings
the magpies gulp

The medicine cabinet of blue and green bottles
is sticky with the its history

the Jurassic era the Triassic era
the Ice Age of her cough

you can listen in the pre-dawn to the pandemonium
of its nightingales, it even converses sometimes

like a fresh batch of parrots. On occasion
it is as ostentatious as a peacock

and always, always, unkind as a raven

In the end there are only two time zones in this world
of your asthmatic child:

1. the cough

2. the absence of the cough

FIELD MARKS

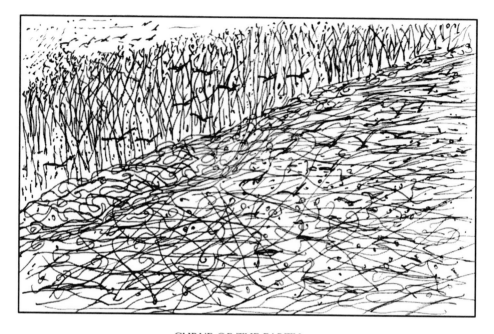

CURVE OF THE EARTH

AND SO

I became determined to
love the smell of things
gone wrong.
To find their beauty,
their broken vacuum cleaner hearts.

A bad carburetor
smells of summer's bloom.
A broken marriage
has the scent of over-cooked meat
and wilted flowers that never mended
anything.

I loved those flowers anyway
and the roots that brought them
up from underground
and the seed packages
with their artistic renditions
and the water they drank all summer
from the hose.

I learned to recycle
arguments into strawberry plants.
Took a string of betrayals
and stitched a quilt.

I could sew broken
promises into patches
for my jacket.

I made a lantern of a few old lies
and was grateful for the light
it lent to the path
through the woods
to my studio of ailments
and the off brand hate
that had been tossed my way.

That is where I go now to manufacture
various iridescent miracles.
I take a handful each day of the newly sprouted
and spread them around
and around
and down, down come the birds.

LO, AND BEHOLD

Look at this:
a red leafed Japanese maple
filled with small blue birds
of an unknown genus.
A whole society of indigo life.

Red tree. Blue birds.
The branches blossoming
with pratter and preen,
An office of similarly clad secretaries,
each set upon some miniscule
and certain task.

There is not enough bandwidth in the world
to record such busy loveliness.
At least a 7.5 on the Richter scale of beauty.
It hurts the heart, really,
this explosion of song,
this flip book of life.

LOUD MIGRATION

METEOROLOGICAL INCIDENT

Shameless, spread eagle,

Marilyn on a steam grate.

We look at YOU, we have to see IT.
Momentous accretion unaddressed, undressed, unwrapped, unwanted

Detritus of detritus, Oh Say Can You See It? Indigo. Violet, Orange.
I need a tissue. Raindrop interloper.

I cry for the whole thing. Color, light, rain, trash.
9/11 Remains. O excellent and dire spot for bird watching.

What is it you want here, double wide spectrum over the Fresh Kills?
Congressional Medal of Honor? Purple Heart? Nobel?

O purple purple purple mountain majesty, assault of opposites,
that lives for minutes and then dies.

It is hard work to see you, to be honest, beauty
and this beast. Afternoon spitting at us

In the atom splitting light.

THE YELLOW

the daisy light
has escaped the garden

lands on the porch with a sun-bang
a pop rock, melted crayon, lemon pie

sunflowers are turning their heads
to see the arc of bright

flown up to the treetops and upon the field
stripes of yellow, flights of yellow

yellow resting on branches and warm yellow on the wires
spilling on the road, the yard

it's been yellow all day in specks and blotches
festooning light   smiling light

confetti of yellow haranguing the grass
yellow in corners and on top of other yellow

and one sun bright sneaker sleeping in the sandbox
somehow left

                                                            behind

THE NORTH COUNTRY

This is where we live now
at the intersection of ice and wind
where cloudbank meets lake
and river leaps like an unleashed dog

Here is where hang our jackets
at the crossroads of vine and moss
where tangled grass
asks the church of spring
for permission to sing in its choir
sing sing and hum and sing
until summer night comes whistling

Here is where we spy the redwinged
and the blue, the brown and black Paridae
the nesting and the ones that merely
come to roost

Because this is where we live now
where we rake up autumn rapture
collect all the old lullabies
and recycle them because this is the again

and again place
where we live now
where we live now
where we live

PLUMAGE

CATCH A PEACOCK

HOW TO CATCH A PEACOCK

every single day
it's glamour shots
for these drag queens
who vogue and bustle
dance up the dust

dress for the opera
in tapestry
and tiaras

they could waken corpses
with their morning songs
they scream like they're on fire

the best known way to catch one
is to chase it into your car

what you will do with it from there –
that is up to you.

BIG DREAMS

ALBINO PEACOCK AT LOS POBLANOS

While you eat your crème brulee,
he is feasting on caterpillars.
While you sip coffee with ouzo,
he is down in the rushes
past the lavender beds, pecking for frogs
the size of your thumb.

Every day he comes out in his finest
and when he chooses, he can open up
his heart like that Mexican
fan dancer in Tepotzlan, twirling in the dust.

Oh, he is a wild one.
Sometimes, late a night, you can spot him
out walking the road.
That cross-dressing bride
of Los Poblanos.
Everyone knows him.

That innocent.
That precious tart.

CLOCK

1.
When I was fifteen I taught myself how to fit into a clock
I hunched my back, pushed my toes into the seconds
pulled my knees to my chin and counted backwards

I practiced until I could sit still inside a minute like a jay
and finally a whole day from sun up 'til down
Like forest owls, I let the ticking synch
with my heartbeat   my breath

2.
When I was sixteen I made myself cozy inside a calendar
spreading my limbs until my feet made it all the way to Sunday
It felt good to fit myself into five days
the way God made the world
and then, I lay myself down for two days
and rested

3.
If I held my breath I later found
I could become anti-time
I could will myself backwards like a fly fisher
or a loon, I could wing back to the smallest
and most insignificant moments:
coffee in the pot, the heel of bread on a table

4.
At twenty two I became a bird

I dug insects from bark
chose my flight pattern

built a nest from found things
scraps of kitchen, tired blankets

I learned to own
my own impressive wingspan

I went all the way to Paraguay
just in time for spring

5.
To this day, I will pick up a chunk of time
put it in my mouth, roll it around, see how it tastes

Sometimes I hold a certain moment under my tongue like a marble

It doesn't have to be an interesting moment or special
I will look hard at any small uncertain bird
and then graft it to my bones, just to prove I can do it
Just to prove I have been alive

THIS IS THE (P)ART

this is this is this is this is this is this is this is this is this is this is this
is this
the part the part the part the part the part the part the part the part the
part the part the part

when the band plays
when the clowns tumble out of the small car
when the thunder claps

when we separate into groups representing like interests
when the dandelions whisper

when the curtain falls
when we bow our heads

when we pray to false idols
when the crows bark

when the brakes screech
this is that part

the part when we scream
and applaud
for the good guys
or the bad guys

this is the part where we all get up
and head for home

THE RED TAILED HAWKS
OF COLESVILLE NEW YORK

They were a couple
And I named them Spunk and Spike

All spring
they cozied up on the telephone wires
over Tunnel Road
Dipping over the railroad
side by side
winging in tandem
or one trailing the other

Then they played switchback
all summer
over the road
people knew about them
"seen them red-tail hawks?" they'd ask
down at the convenience store

The next year
it was only Spunk
over the road
in its loosestrife dress

And then he, too, disappeared

MIGRATION

BIRD SPIRALS

INFINITE

This, the reflection in the rear view mirror
of the sky reflected in the lake

This, the Native American woman on Land-O-Lakes
butter, holding a box of Land-O-Lakes

Butter, with herself, holding another
butter. This, the way we held one another

The night the rain funneled into the river
which went to another river

that went to the sea
where we wanted to sail

To see Elvez, the Mexican Elvis, sing
of blue suede shoes, and dance away our blues

This, the white on white migratory pattern
of terns, that repeats annually, pole to pole

This, Aunt Stella's dog, McGee
named in honor of her last dog, McGee

and her very first McGee, who jumped into the sea
to chase the moon, bouncing on the mirror

Of water, that came from the river
Blue

As the memory of a dreamed-of lake
a ghost lake

one hazel eye
staring up at the terns

and back at us
again

ARCTIC TERN

Michael Faris' dad, Frank,
sat out back with his 22 gauge rifle
knocking off prairie dogs
on those summer evenings
in the warm watermelon light of the North Valley.
"Damn Rats!" he'd swear.

All his life he'd held the upper hand.
Ex-sheriff, Indian trader, in Lebanese and Spanish
he'd pipe orders –
at the Christmas tree lot in December
and the Fireworks stand before the 4th of July.

He was, you could say, a memorable man,
who knew how to hang a cigarette
off a bottom lip like it belonged there.

He knew a thing or two about existentialism, too.
Whenever it was time to get milk
Or shop for food,
Or get some gas, he would say the same thing:

Let's go out, so we can come back again.

HALF PAST BLUEJAY

On the clock
of birds

it is half past
bluejay

a quarter to
the white throated sparrows

later, it will be
dark-eyed dunces

all around
for hours

LAST BIRD OF THE DAY

It has to do with the way it flings, madly
like a shot punctuation mark

It has to do with the way it leaps branches and telephone wires
to ride the air to an invisible height

It has to do with the tilt-a-whirl of feathers
and with the aria you know is sleeping in its throat

This is why you follow it with your eyes, as you sit before
the red light at Prospect and Broad Streets

in Plattsburgh, New York
the afternoon your great aunt Esther Greene

is celebrating her 104th birthday in Cleveland, Ohio
Sit too long, watching

until it becomes a comma in the clouds
the period yet to be placed

at the end of her phenomenal days
It has to do with each syllable of bird that has passed

through your life
in the book of phenomenal birds you have known

IDENTIFIABLE MARKINGS

MIGRATING BIRDS RESTING

LATIN NAMES OF BIRDS
AND BINOMIAL NOMENCLATURE

follow language to its roots
and find birds

perched on their nouns
like the stuffed birds

at the Museum of Natural History
wearing their root clothes

and elaborate root hats
full of the ancient taste

words have when pressed
to the tongue

by history
Avis, ave: taste of sunlight

on feathers
and mysterious dinosaur

wingspans
taste like stone soup

soup of bones
some make you feel better

like Cathartes aura
and some might make you smile

(Turdus migratorius)
others still

roll out of your mouth
like charming music

played on zithers
Columba livia

Zanaida macouvre
names fancy as ball gowns

at the annual gathering
of the ornithologists

where Mimus polyglottus
and Curvus brachyrhynocus

might sip champagne
and compare notes on migration

all this is set forth in the
International Code of Zoological Nomenclature

Where all things
have two names

one to connect them
to other creatures

one just to call their own

HISTORICAL PATTERNS OF AVIAN TAXONOMY

follow the drift and jetsam
of the many species
on the updraft of nice typography

in this fat book
in which this one grows an orange proboscis
that one, a tail
like a Chinese fan dancer

this is what Darwin loved:
the ways they merged and separated
to meet the world

like debutantes
dressing for different balls
they try on every shape of fluted beak
--what is in style
in Micronesia and Java
is so different from the Floridian peninsula

they fly through the pages
doves on the grey days, little tit
and magpie in snow pastures

wearing their Latin names
like badges of importance
As if to say *science loves me*

I am Graculus, like a Caesar
the Northern Pintail is Anas Acuta

The seafaring birds
are "pelagics"
which sounds like medicine
for skin abrasions

Or something you give your dog
when he loses interest in life
to make him get out there
and go at it again

THE MAYBE

falls from the sky
in a heap

with determination
down onto

the smallest rodent
--a mole or mouse—

a heat seeking
missile of bird

it hits its mark
and leaves

it was a maybe bird
maybe from the north

maybe heading south
maybe a hawk

maybe not
we could not decide

it was too fast
and too maybe

it wore its maybe
feathers

like any other bird
it had no identifiable markings

it was here and then gone
and it scooped its maybe prey

maybe someday
it will come back

MOLTING SEASON

Seven contour feathers
on the banks of the clear ditch
behind Bosque Farms

cluster of polka dots and stripes
some guinea hen
tossed off

as she strutted
on her way to another place
over there maybe

or back behind
It is the time for that
Seasonal molting

Think of it
as a gift
and take them home

BIRDS, BIRDS, BIRDS

What do they want from the world, the birds?

Small sticks
mud
fluff from dandelions
worms
corn silk
teensy baby grasshoppers

Water in puddles, lakes, the wide seas

One another

You can tell by their persistent call and response at dawn
the pairing off on wires
The collectives they form to debate at dusk
The patterns they make in those jumbo square dance-a-thons

They can fill the auditorium of the sky with their dancing
then cover the ground like a sleepy, feathered tarp

Even if they are sad, the birds are the happiness of the world
Even if they are sad, they will not tell you

ABOUT THE AUTHOR

Elizabeth Cohen is an English professor at Plattsburgh State University/SUNY, where she teaches creative writing and serves as co-editor of the Saranac Review. She holds an MFA from Columbia University and is the author of four previous books and chapbooks of poetry; a book of short stories, *The Hypothetical Girl*; and a memoir, *The Family on Beartown Road*, among other publications. Her poems, articles, stories, and essays have appeared in Northwest Review, Exquisite Corpse, Ellipses, Yale Review, SELF, MORE, Newsweek, People, Rolling Stone, The New York Times Magazine, Tablet, and other publications.

To learn more, please go to www.elizabethcohen.me.

ABOUT THE ARTIST

Aliki Barnstone is a poet, translator, critic, editor, and visual artist. Her visual art has appeared in *New Letters* and *Tiferet*. She is the author of eight books of poetry, most recently, *Dwelling* (Sheep Meadow, 2016), *Bright Body* (White Pine, 2011) and *Dear God Dear, Dr. Heartbreak: New and Selected Poems* (Sheep Meadow, 2009), and the translator of *The Collected Poems of C.P. Cavafy: A New Translation* (W.W. Norton, 2006). Her first book of poems, *The Real Tin Flower* (Crowell-Collier, 1968), was published when she was 12 years old, with a forward by Anne Sexton. In 2014, Carnegie-Mellon University Press reissued her book, *Madly in Love*, as a Carnegie-Mellon Classic Contemporary.

Her awards include a Senior Fulbright Fellowship in Greece, the Silver Pen Award from the Nevada Writers Hall of Fame, Pennsylvania Council on the Arts Literature Fellowship in Poetry, and a residency at the Anderson Center at Tower View. She serves as Poet Laureate of Missouri and is Professor of English and Creative Writing at the University of Missouri.

To learn more, please go to www.alikibarnstone.com.

BIRD TREE

ACKNOWLEDGEMENTS

Festival of the Cranes and *Pond Cam* published in Tallow Eider Quarterly, 2016.

Bird Elixir and *Lo, and Behold-* published in Exquisite Corpse, 2010

The Yes – published in Hawaii Pacific Review, 2015, Nominated for "Best of the Net" and Pushcart prizes

Clock – published in riverSedge: A Journal of Art and Literature, 2015

The Afterlife of Birds, Water, Poem of Sex and Time, Second Poem of Sex and Time, and *The North Country*, published in NYU's Black Renaissance Noire, 2015

Area Codes, published in The Road Not Taken: A Journal of Formal Poetry, 2016

Lo, and Behold and *Blue Bird*, published in the chapbook *Mother Love*, Keshet Press, 2009

Note to reader: Some "found" comments taken from the Cornell Lab of Ornithology web site.

CPSIA information can be obtained at www.ICGtesting.com
Printed in the USA
LVOW08s0920191016

509353LV00001B/2/P